PODCASTERS

BY ABBY BADACH DOYLE

Gareth Stevens
PUBLISHING

Please visit our website, www.garethstevens.com. For a free color catalog of all our high-quality books, call toll free 1-800-542-2595 or fax 1-877-542-2596.

Cataloging-in-Publication Data

Names: Doyle, Abby Badach.
Title: Podcasters / Abby Badach Doyle.
Description: New York : Gareth Stevens Publishing, 2020. | Series: Digital insiders | Includes glossary and index.
Identifiers: ISBN 9781538247594 (pbk.) | ISBN 9781538247617 (library bound) | ISBN 9781538247600 (6 pack)
Subjects: LCSH: Podcasting–Juvenile literature.
Classification: LCC TK5105.887 D69 2020 | DDC 006.7′876–dc23

First Edition

Published in 2020 by
Gareth Stevens Publishing
111 East 14th Street, Suite 349
New York, NY 10003

Copyright © 2020 Gareth Stevens Publishing

Designer: Sarah Liddell
Editor: Lynn Moon

Photo credits: Cover, p. 1 Ruslan Guzov/Shutterstock.com; background texture used throughout VLADGRIN/Shutterstock.com; screen texture used throughout majcot/Shutterstock.com; p. 5 (top) David MG/Shutterstock.com; p. 5 (bottom) sirikorn thamniyom/Shutterstock.com; p. 7 Kim Kulish/Contributor/Corbis Historical/Getty Images; p. 11 wavebreakmedia/Shutterstock.com; p. 13 (top) Yuriy Golub/Shutterstock.com; p. 13 (bottom) Denys Prykhodov/Shutterstock.com; p. 15 HBRH/Shutterstock.com; p. 19 Marko Poplasen/Shutterstock.com; p. 21 (top) PrinceOfLove/Shutterstock.com; p. 21 (bottom) New Africa/Shutterstock.com; p. 23 Rawpixel.com/Shutterstock.com; p. 25 Monkey Business Images/Shutterstock.com; p. 27 (top) Matthew Eisman/Contributor/Getty Images Entertainment/Getty Images; p. 27 (bottom) VALERIE MACON/Contributor/AFP/Getty Images; p. 29 Syda Productions/Shutterstock.com.

Printed in the United States of America

Some of the images in this book illustrate individuals who are models. The depictions do not imply actual situations or events.

CPSIA compliance information: Batch #CW20GS: For further information contact Gareth Stevens, New York, New York at 1-800-542-2595.

CONTENTS

Words in the glossary appear in **bold** type the first time they are used in the text.

WELCOME TO PODCASTING

It's fun to get lost in a good story. With podcasts, you can explore and listen to millions of interesting stories ... all at your fingertips! Whether you like science, music, sports, or mysteries, there's a podcast for almost every interest. Better yet, you can **subscribe** to your favorites and listen on your own time.

Maybe you've heard of podcasts, but aren't sure how to start listening. Perhaps you dream of hosting a famous podcast of your own. Want to know what it's really like in the recording studio? Let's go behind the scenes of this popular **medium** to find out!

🔍 WHAT'S IN A NAME?

The term podcast was first used in 2004 and comes from the words "iPod" and "**broadcast**." Before that, podcasts were sometimes called "audio blogs." Audio refers to sound and a blog is a website where someone posts content. When two words are squished together to form a new word, it's called a portmanteau.

THERE ARE MORE THAN 550,000 PODCASTS
AVAILABLE ON ITUNES ALONE, WITH
NEW ONES BEING ADDED EVERY DAY!

HOW IT BEGAN

In the early 2000s, website makers wondered if they could make a blog using sound clips instead of just text and pictures. Blogger Dave Winer figured out the technology in 2004. Then, TV star Adam Curry made "audio blogs" popular with his show *Daily Source Code*. The podcast was born!

By 2005, more than 3,000 free podcasts were on iTunes. People would download podcasts at home, then listen on an iPod. When the iPhone was made public in 2008, it got easier to download audio files on the go. Podcasts became so popular by 2014 that Apple included its podcast app on all iPhones.

THIS IS NPR

National Public Radio (NPR) has been broadcasting on US **airwaves** for more than 50 years. They have long been seen as experts in telling attention-grabbing stories using only sound. Today, NPR also produces dozens of popular podcasts, like *Up First* and *Fresh Air*. About 19 million people listen to their podcasts every month!

ADAM CURRY, SOMETIMES CALLED "THE PODFATHER," REACHED MORE THAN 500,000 SUBSCRIBERS ON HIS POPULAR PODCAST *DAILY SOURCE CODE*.

FIND YOUR FAVORITES

Podcasts are released as episodes, or chapters, of a program that centers on a theme. Most people listen on a smartphone. You could also listen on a computer, smart watch, or in the car. Special apps let you search for and subscribe to podcasts you like. These are sometimes called "podcatchers."

Popular podcatchers include Apple Podcasts, Spotify, Google Play Music, Pocket Casts, and Overcast. A podcatcher can notify you when a new episode is ready. You can then **stream** episodes, or download them and listen offline. It's okay to unsubscribe to a podcast if you aren't interested anymore. With so many to choose from, you're sure to find one you like!

ASK FOR PERMISSION

Remember to ask a trusted adult before you use the internet. Just like movies and TV shows, some podcasts talk about things that aren't okay for kids. These are usually marked with a tag that says "explicit." Tell an adult if you see or hear something online that makes you uncomfortable.

PODCASTS FOR KIDS

SCIENCE

Wow in the World
Brains On!
But Why: A Podcast For Curious Kids
Tumble Science Podcast for Kids

NEWS AND INTERVIEWS

KidNuz
Eleanor Amplified
Dream Big Podcast

MUSIC

Ear Snacks
Spare the Rock, Spoil the Child

STORIES

Story Pirates
Peace Out
What If World
Story Time
Storynory

GOOD QUESTIONS

Short and Curly
Five Minutes with Dad

CHECK OUT THESE POPULAR KID-FRIENDLY PODCASTS ONLINE OR THROUGH YOUR FAVORITE PODCAST APP. YOU CAN ALSO ASK A TEACHER OR LIBRARIAN TO SUGGEST A FEW TOO.

HOW TO START A PODCAST

To start a podcast, you need to answer one simple but big question: What's your show about? Some podcasts talk about the latest in news, sports, movies, or music. Others share jokes, perform short plays, or tell ghost stories! Your podcast can be about anything, but it helps to have a theme.

You will also need to pick a format, or a structure, that makes your episodes feel the same. Some podcasts are long. Some are short. Some feel like chatting with your friends at lunch. Others are more formal. Many podcasts have a host who interviews, or asks questions of, different guests.

🔍 WHO'S IN CHARGE?

Traditional radio, like AM and FM stations, has to follow certain rules. The Federal Communications Commission issues broadcast licenses, or permits, and makes rules for the airwaves. For example, radio stations can't advertise tobacco or say certain swear words. Since podcasts are published online, they don't have to follow those rules.

A HOST IS THE MAIN SPEAKER ON A PODCAST. A PRODUCER DOES WORK BEHIND THE SCENES, LIKE EDITING SOUND OR FINDING INFORMATION FOR THE SHOW.

After you choose a theme and format, you still have a few things to decide. How often will your episodes be released? With a podcast, you can be **flexible**. Many podcasts have new episodes every week, but you don't have to record that often if you don't want to.

Finally, choose a title for your podcast. When you find one you like, search online to see if it's already taken. You will also want to claim your title as a website and on **social media**. Want to test if your title is catchy enough? Tell a friend, then have them guess what your show is about!

🔍 HOSTING AND RSS

To share your podcast with the world, you need a place to host, or store, it online. Popular hosting options include SoundCloud, Anchor, Buzzsprout and Podbean. Your hosting site will give you a special web address called an RSS feed. An RSS feed is how you **distribute** your show to podcatchers like iTunes and Spotify.

RSS STANDS FOR "REALLY SIMPLE SYNDICATION." IN OTHER WORDS, IT'S AN EASY WAY TO SEND YOUR PODCAST TO MANY PLACES, LIKE ITUNES AND SPOTIFY, AT THE SAME TIME.

GET YOUR GEAR

Now that you have an idea for your podcast, you can think about how to record it. **Professional** podcasters might have big recording studios with expensive microphones and other equipment, or gear. You can find a good microphone for less than $100 to use at home. For a quick setup, you just need a smartphone and a computer! A good pair of headphones helps too.

Many smartphones come with a voice recorder app. On the iPhone, it's called Voice Memos. You can find it in an iPhone's Utilities folder. If your phone doesn't come with one, you can download an app like Easy Voice Recorder.

🔍 AM I OLD ENOUGH?

Some apps and websites have age restrictions, or limits, on who is allowed to sign up for an account or use the service. For example, Apple's Podcasts app and Anchor only allow users ages 13 and up. If you're not old enough yet, you can still listen or record with a trusted adult.

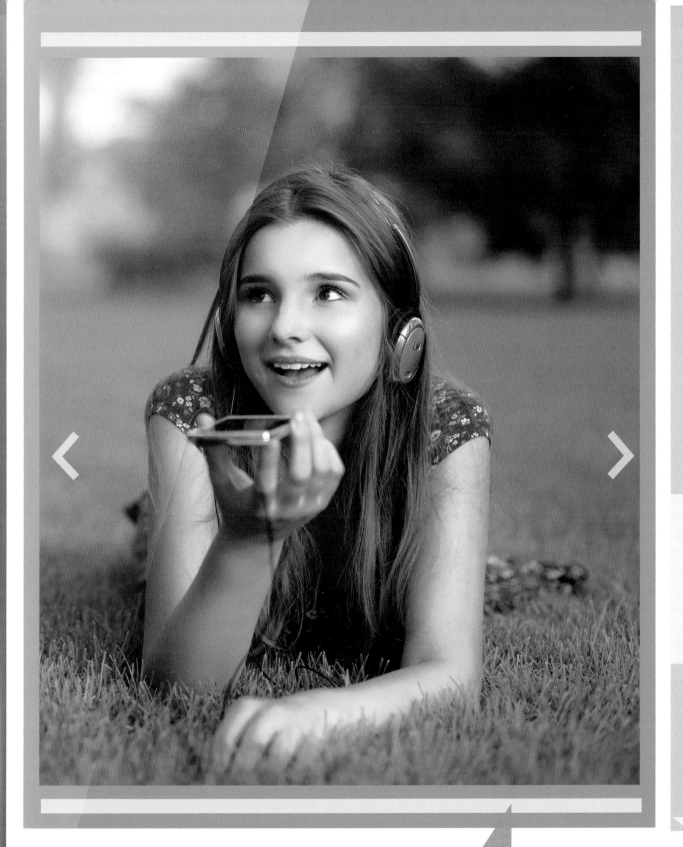

RECORDINGS CAN TAKE UP A LOT OF MEMORY. IF
YOU USE YOUR SMARTPHONE TO RECORD, MAKE SURE
TO CHECK THAT YOU HAVE ENOUGH STORAGE!

A podcast is usually pieced together using little bits of sound, like interviews with a guest or pieces of music. That's why you need a computer with sound editing software. The **software** will let you piece together your "audio," which is what the pros call those little bits of sound. The process of editing audio is called "mixing."

Apple devices like Macbooks come with the sound editing program GarageBand. Another popular choice is Audacity (aw-DASS-a-tee), which you can download for free online. Many professionals use Adobe Audition, but it costs money and has a lot of extra features you don't need as a beginner.

🔍 HOW LONG?

Traditional TV and radio shows have to be a specific length. For example, the news might come on at 6 p.m. and last exactly 1 hour. But with podcasts, every episode can be different! Research shows that most episodes average around 45 minutes. However, many are longer or shorter.

NEW PODCAST CHECKLIST

☐ CHOOSE A THEME AND FORMAT

☐ PICK A TITLE

☐ MAKE WEBSITE AND SOCIAL MEDIA PROFILES

☐ SELECT HOSTING SERVICE

☐ GATHER EQUIPMENT:
   SMARTPHONE OR MICROPHONE
   COMPUTER
   EDITING SOFTWARE
   HEADPHONES

☐ PLAN YOUR FIRST FEW EPISODES:
   THINGS TO TALK ABOUT
   GUESTS TO INTERVIEW
   LENGTH OF EPISODES
   HOW OFTEN YOU'LL RELEASE EPISODES

WHEN STARTING A BRAND-NEW PODCAST, IT HELPS TO PLAN AHEAD. HERE IS A LIST OF IMPORTANT THINGS TO DO OR THINK ABOUT BEFORE YOU RECORD YOUR FIRST EPISODE.

RECORDING AND EDITING

You planned your show. You have your gear. Now, it's time to record! Start by finding a quiet location. You want a spot with very little background noise, such as a ticking clock or traffic zipping by. Even a refrigerator makes a low hum that could show up on your recording!

To record, hold your smartphone a few inches away from your mouth. Then press the big red "record" button. Practice your setup and play your audio back to make sure it sounds good. If you're too close, it might sound scratchy. If you're too far away, it might sound weak.

SETTING THE SCENE

Sometimes, background noise can help set the scene! Pros call this ambience, or "nat" (natural) sound. Imagine you're at a farm. You might hear animal noises, windchimes, or a tractor driving by. If you're on location, record at least a minute of nat sound to mix in if you need it.

PROFESSIONAL STUDIOS OFTEN HAVE FOAM ON THE WALLS. THIS CONTROLS THE SOUND, REDUCES ECHOES, AND MAKES THE RECORDINGS SOUND CLEARER.

If you are interviewing a guest, do some background research first. That way, you can ask better questions and get better answers. Dig deep! Avoid questions that can be answered with a simple "yes" or "no."

After recording, it's time to edit. This can take a while, so be patient! When you edit, you arrange audio clips to tell an interesting story—even if they didn't originally happen in that order. Once you create the structure, the final step is to mix. Mixing is about smoothing out the details, like making sure the loudness of each clip is the same.

🔍 DO I REALLY TALK LIKE THAT!?

Why does your voice sound different on a recording? When you talk, sound waves **vibrate** the bones in your head. That makes your voice sound deeper... but only to you! When you listen to a recording, the sound travels through the air. That makes your voice sound higher or "thinner" than you're used to.

A PAIR OF HIGH-QUALITY HEADPHONES CAN HELP YOU HEAR TINY (BUT IMPORTANT!) PROBLEMS IN YOUR MIX, LIKE BREATHS OR POPS OF AIR.

IS ANYONE LISTENING?

Professional podcasters want to know how many people are listening to their show. Computer programs can track how many times an episode is streamed or downloaded. However, sometimes the same person could be counted more than once if they started streaming an episode in one location (like at home) and streamed the rest somewhere else (like the gym).

Other important things to measure include visits to your website, your number of social media followers, and how many people share your content. The number of subscribers your show has tells you how many people are getting an update whenever there is a new episode.

🔍 LARGER AUDIENCE = MORE MONEY

In general, the bigger your audience, the more you can charge companies to advertise with you. This is true in almost all media—not just podcasts! For example, it usually costs more to buy an ad in a national magazine like *People* than it does in a small local newspaper.

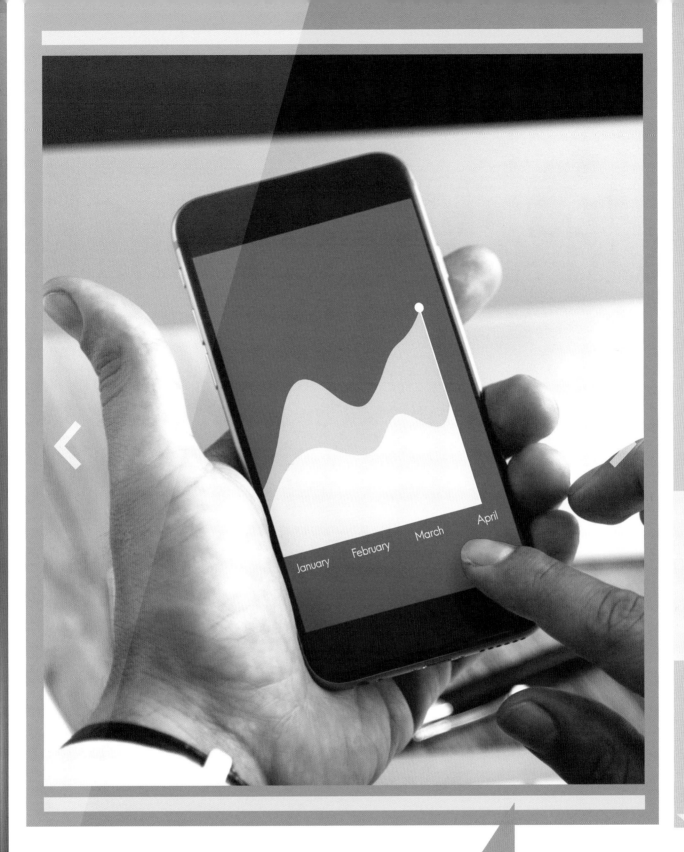

KEEP TRACK OF DOWNLOADS TO SEE WHICH EPISODES YOUR AUDIENCE, OR LISTENERS, LIKE THE MOST. THEN YOU CAN PLAN BETTER SHOWS!

ADS AND SPONSORS

How do podcasts make money? The answer is the same way many radio and TV programs do: by selling advertisements. However, podcast ads often feel a little more personal than traditional ads. Podcast listeners trust their favorite hosts, so these ads are powerful and effective.

One popular style of ad is an endorsement. This is when a host personally speaks about a product (like clothes) or service (like a meal delivery plan) they use in real life. Since the ad is delivered by a familiar voice, these ads also feel more natural than a "traditional" commercial that interrupts the show's flow.

🔍 TRACKING WHAT YOU BUY

How can companies tell if their podcast ads are working? One way is promo codes. A podcast host might tell listeners to use "Code 123" when they shop online. If the store sees a lot of people using that special code at checkout, they know the audience is listening—and buying!

THE ADVERTISING COMPANY MIDROLL STATES THAT
61 PERCENT OF THEIR LISTENERS REPORTED BEING MORE LIKELY
TO BUY SOMETHING AFTER HEARING AN AD ON THEIR PODCASTS.
MIDROLL PODCAST HOSTS READ THE ADS THEMSELVES.

CAREERS IN PODCASTING

Many podcasters run their shows just for fun. However, it's possible to have a full-time career in podcasting. To learn the basics, it helps to have a college degree in communications, journalism, or media arts.

You can work on-air as a host, or behind the scenes as a producer or editor. Some jobs have you do both. You could also work in podcast advertising or sales. Podcasts need money from ads and sponsors, or companies that can give money in return for advertising. Could you see yourself working at a big media company like NPR, iHeartRadio, or ESPN? Remember, every famous voice got their start somewhere. Dream big!

🔍 PODCAST AWARDS

Musicians have the Grammy Awards. Actors have the Academy Awards. Podcasting is still a young medium, but the pros have created awards to recognize each others' success. These include The People's Choice Podcast Awards, the Webby Awards, the iHeartRadio Podcast Awards, and the Academy of Podcasters Awards.

IRA GLASS

OPRAH WINFREY

IRA GLASS IS THE HOST AND LEAD PRODUCER OF
THIS AMERICAN LIFE, A POPULAR RADIO SHOW AND PODCAST.
OPRAH WINFREY IS A TELEVISION HOST AND ACTOR WHO
NOW HOSTS THE PODCAST *SUPERSOUL CONVERSATIONS.*

WHAT'S NEXT?

New technology makes it easier than ever to listen to podcasts. You can ask a smart speaker like Alexa, Google Home, or Siri to play your favorites. Many new smart devices "talk" to each other too. If you listen at home, now you can pick up where you left off in the car!

Whether it's podcasts, movies, or TV, today's audiences prefer to catch their favorite shows on their own terms. Podcasts have become more popular over the past 10 years with no signs of slowing down. Today, about one in four people in the US over age 12 listens monthly. Tune in and join the fun!

🔍 SUPPORT YOUR FAVORITE PODCASTS

Many podcasters work hard at what they do and like to hear from fans. Send your favorite show a message through email or social media. If your favorite podcast is made by a **nonprofit**, like NPR or a local public radio station, you could also give money to help keep the show running.

PROFESSIONALS FIGURE ABOUT 73 MILLION AMERICANS OVER AGE 12 LISTEN TO PODCASTS AT LEAST ONCE PER MONTH. THAT'S UP FROM 67 MILLION PEOPLE IN 2017.

GLOSSARY

airwaves: the signals used to send out radio and television programs

broadcast: to send out by radio, television, or computer

distribute: to give or deliver to people

flexible: easily changed

medium: a system of communication, such as newspapers, radio, or television

nonprofit: an organization that is not run for the sake of making a profit

professional: having to do with a job someone does for a living. Also, someone who does a job that requires special training, skills, or education.

social media: forms of electronic communication that allow people to create online communities to share ideas, send personal messages, and share information

software: a computer code, or program, that performs certain functions

stream: to transfer data in a continuous way meant to be watched or listened to immediately

subscribe: to get a publication or service regularly

traditional: having to do with long-practiced customs

vibrate: to rapidly move back and forth or from side to side

FOR MORE INFORMATION

BOOKS

Anniss, Matthew. *Create Your Own Podcast*. North Mankato, MN: Heinemann Raintree, 2017.

Higgins, Nadia. *Making a Podcast*. Mankato, MN: Amicus Ink, 2018.

Hudak, Heather C. *Creative Podcast Producers*. Minneapolis, MN: Checkerboard Library, 2019

WEBSITES

Kids Listen
www.kidslisten.org
This nonprofit group makes it easy to discover kid-friendly podcasts for your age and interests. They also have a free app to download.

Kids' Rules for Online Safety
www.safekids.com/kids-rules-for-online-safety
This list gives parents and kids some topics to talk about regarding safe internet use.

NPR Training
https://training.npr.org/
The pros from National Public Radio put together these beginners' guides to storytelling, mixing audio, and more.

INDEX